CALIFORNIA
MISSIONS

Discovering Mission San Luis Rey de Francia

BY JEANNETTE BUCKLEY

Cavendish
Square

New York

Published in 2015 by Cavendish Square Publishing, LLC
243 5th Avenue, Suite 136, New York, NY 10016

CPSIA Compliance Information: Batch #WS14CSQ

All websites were available and accurate when this book was sent to press.

Library of Congress Cataloging-in-Publication Data

Buckley, Jeannette.
Discovering Mission San Luis Rey de Francia / Jeannette Buckley.
pages cm. — (California missions)
Includes index.
ISBN 978-1-62713-112-4 (hardcover) ISBN 978-1-62713-114-8 (ebook)
1. San Luis Rey Mission (Calif.)—History—Juvenile literature. 2. Spanish mission buildings—California—Oceanside—History—Juvenile literature. 3. Franciscans—California—Oceanside—History—Juvenile literature. 4. California—History—To 1846—Juvenile literature. 5. Luiseño Indians—Missions—California Oceanside—History—Juvenile literature. I. Title.
F869.S397B83 2015
979.4'98—dc23
2014010503

Editorial Director: Dean Miller
Editor: Kristen Susienka
Copy Editor: Cynthia Roby
Art Director: Jeffrey Talbot
Designer: Douglas Brooks
Photo Researcher: J8 Media
Production Manager: Jennifer Ryder-Talbot
Production Editor: David McNamara

Printed in the United States of America

CALIFORNIA
MISSIONS

Contents

Mission San Luis Rey de Francia, known as "the King of Missions," was named after King Louis IX. He was taught by the Franciscans and died during the Crusades in the thirteenth century.

1
Discovering a New World

THE KING OF MISSIONS

Outside Oceanside, California, is a peaceful retreat. Here, a white bell tower stretches into the blue sky. This tranquil sanctuary is the location of Mission San Luis Rey de Francia. Referred to as "the King of the Missions," it was founded in the 1700s by Spanish **friars**, or *frays*, and soldiers and built by members of the Luiseño tribe. Raised from humble beginnings, the mission has stood for centuries, becoming a symbol of the important history of California.

THE SPANISH ARRIVE IN THE AMERICAS

Although Mission San Luis Rey de Francia was not founded until 1798, its story began much earlier. In 1493, Christopher Columbus brought back news of his findings in the Americas to Spain. Europeans had never been there before, and they decided to explore the area further, hoping to discover gold, great cities to conquer, or a faster trade route to Asia.

In 1521, a Spanish explorer named Hernán Cortés conquered the great Aztec empire for Spain. He renamed the land New Spain—today known as Mexico—and set up a government under

Cabrillo was an explorer who came to the New World to claim land for Spain.

an official called a **viceroy**, who would act in place of the king. In 1542, Viceroy Mendoza of New Spain sent an explorer named Juan Rodríguez Cabrillo up the Pacific Coast to look for a river that would cut through North America to Asia.

Cabrillo did not find this river. Instead, he found the harbor that is known today as San Diego Bay, and eagerly shared this information upon his return to New Spain. However, since Cabrillo hadn't found riches, the viceroy didn't think it was worth the money and effort it would cost to send more ships there. The Spanish would not return to the place they called *Alta*, or "upper," California for many years.

Eventually, other European nations explored California, including the Russians, who were very interested in settling Alta California. When the Spanish heard about this, they decided to send settlers to the area in order to retain the land they had claimed. On January 7, 1769, the first of three ships set sail for the San Diego harbor Cabrillo had found more than 200 years earlier. Four months later, on May 15, a group of men began their journey on horseback over land to meet the ships. The first Spanish colonists had arrived in Alta California.

2
The Luiseño

LIFE BEFORE THE MISSIONS

Native people had lived in Alta California for thousands of years. Each group, or tribe, lived in a certain space of land, called a territory, and had its own language, beliefs, and customs. The Spanish called the people who lived in the area around the mission the Luiseño, after the mission's namesake, Saint Louis. Prior to their arrival, the Luiseño civilization thrived, but the Spanish colonization of California would change the Luiseño way of life forever.

The Luiseño culture was one deeply rooted in nature, much like that of other Native Californians. Their homes were made of bowed tree branches covered with mud, and they did their cooking outdoors. The men wore little or no clothing, and the women wore aprons that tied around the waist and had panels that hung down in front and back. The Luiseño crafted sandals from yucca tree fibers, which they wore for long journeys. When it was cold, everyone covered themselves with warm capes made of animal fur.

Many Natives lived in thriving communities.

FINDING FOOD

Men, as the primary hunters, were responsible for finding food for their families and other tribe members. They used wooden bows and arrows, which were strung with rope woven from flax and hemp. Their arrowheads were made of hard stone, chipped to form a sharp point. Feathers were attached to the shafts of the arrows to make them fly straight toward their targets. The Luiseño ate the meat of the animals they hunted, and used the skin and feathers as clothing or decoration.

Luiseño men also fished for food. They built wooden boats that were similar to canoes, called *pauhits*, which were used for both fishing and travel. Fish were caught with spears or with nets that the Luiseño fashioned out of handwoven rope.

The Luiseño respected nature and used resources around them to make tools for cooking and hunting.

LUISEÑO CUISINE

The women of the tribe traditionally prepared the family's meals, and gathered seeds, grasses, acorns, and berries to eat.

Acorns, a staple of the Luiseño diet, were used to make a kind of porridge and to make breads. Luiseño women knocked the acorns from oak tree branches with large sticks, gathered them in baskets, and laid them out to dry in the sun. Acorns contain a bitter acid, and cannot be eaten right away. The women ground them between two stones, called a mortar and pestle, and then poured boiling water over the crushed acorns ten times. This process removed the acid, making the acorns ready for cooking.

Cave and rock paintings drawn by the Luiseño still exist today.

YOUNG LUISEÑO

Luiseño boys and girls learned from their parents and other tribe members. Once they were old enough to share some of their tribe's responsibilities, such as hunting, gathering, or caring for younger family members, they took on some of these important jobs themselves.

SKILLED ARTISANS

The Luiseño painted rocks and the walls of nearby caves. The paints they used were made from mixtures of crushed berries, clays, and dried herbs. Using sticks as brushes, they created pictures of the life around them.

They made beautiful necklaces and bracelets from shells and stones they found at the beach. They would also decorate themselves with feathers.

SPIRITUALITY

The Luiseño believed in a single god called Chinigchinish, who watched over them and would punish or reward them for their actions. They also believed in an afterlife, where they would be rewarded for leading a good life, or punished for leading a bad one.

The Luiseño held ceremonies in a building called a *wamkish*. There, the Luiseño celebrated many events, including births, deaths, and when boys and girls became adults. Members of the tribe would gather at a wamkish to sing and dance. Before the Spanish arrived, the peaceful Luiseño thrived for hundreds of years.

Descendants of the Luiseño carry on ancient traditions and customs every year.

3 The Mission System

THE EUROPEAN WORLDVIEW

When the Spanish established New Spain, they realized that colonizing the area was easier if they set up missions where religious leaders could teach the **indigenous people** about **Christianity** and Spanish culture. By making the Native Californians Spanish citizens, it would pave the way for other settlers to come to the land.

Europeans brought many new ideas and diseases to the New World.

Most Europeans at this point in history did not value cultural diversity. They believed that their religion and way of life were superior to those of the Native Californians, and that they needed help to become more "civilized." They also believed that they could take away the indigenous peoples' land. Today, we know that all cultures are important and should be respected. Although the Spanish may have believed at the time that they were helping the Native Californians, European colonization of the Americas drastically changed the course of entire civilizations by bringing diseases that killed entire communities and building missions which threatened the Native way of life.

In order to make the newly conquered territory truly Spanish, it needed to be filled with Spanish people. Since not many people in Spain wanted to go to the Americas, the government sent a few Spanish people to encourage the Native Californians to become

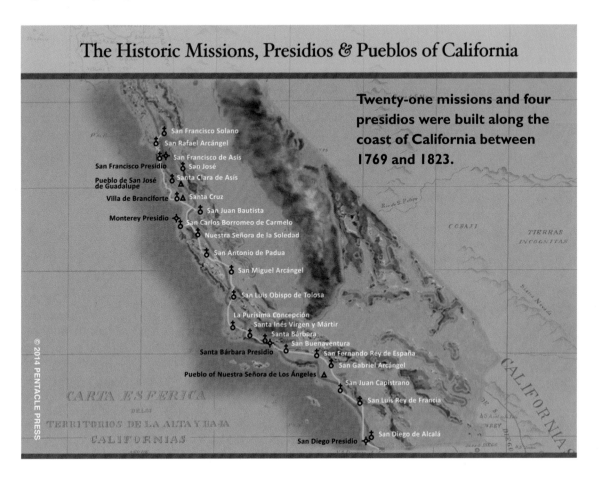

The Historic Missions, Presidios & Pueblos of California

Twenty-one missions and four presidios were built along the coast of California between 1769 and 1823.

San Francisco Solano
San Rafael Arcángel
San Francisco de Asís
San Francisco Presidio
San José
Pueblo de San José de Guadalupe
Santa Clara de Asís
Villa de Branciforte
Santa Cruz
San Juan Bautista
Monterey Presidio
San Carlos Borromeo de Carmelo
Nuestra Señora de la Soledad
San Antonio de Padua
San Miguel Arcángel
San Luis Obispo de Tolosa
La Purísima Concepción
Santa Inés Virgen y Mártir
Santa Bárbara
San Buenaventura
Santa Bárbara Presidio
San Fernando Rey de España
San Gabriel Arcángel
Pueblo of Nuestra Señora de Los Ángeles
San Juan Capistrano
San Luis Rey de Francia
San Diego de Alcalá
San Diego Presidio

Spanish citizens. There were two mission systems: one, started much earlier, was in *Baja,* or "lower," California, and the other was in Alta California.

The missions of Alta California were begun by the **Franciscan** friars and the Spanish military. Friars and soldiers traveled to a mission site together. The friars would **convert** the Native people. The soldiers were sent to protect the friars and manage the mission's workers, who would build the mission as well as a *presidio,* or fort, nearby. There were four forts built along the coast.

THE MISSIONS OF ALTA CALIFORNIA

Between 1769 and 1823, the Spanish built missions in Alta California. The costal area where most missions were constructed was chosen for its proximity to many Native tribes, as well as its rich soil for planting crops and feeding livestock. It was also close to the ocean for fishing.

Fray Junípero Serra was the first leader of the Alta California missions.

The first mission, San Diego de Alcalá, was established by mission president Fray Junípero Serra in 1769. By the time Mission San Luis Rey de Francia was founded in 1798, Fray Serra had died and his successor, Fray Fermín Francisco de Lasuén, had taken over. Mission San Luis Rey de Francia became one of the most successful missions in the Alta California mission system.

4
The Beginnings of the Mission

CHOOSING A LOCATION

While Mission San Luis Rey de Francia was not founded until 1798, the area where it would be built had been recommended as a mission site nearly thirty years earlier.

In 1769, Fray Juan Crespí, one of the first Spanish friars to arrive in California from New Spain, accompanied explorer Gaspar de Portolá and Fray Serra on an expedition to establish bases and missions from San Diego to Monterey. They came upon a green valley five miles (8 kilometers) east of the Pacific Ocean. Amazed by the beauty of the land, Fray Crespí decided it was a gift from God and recommended it as a site for a mission.

The valley's beautiful landscape convinced friars to one day build a mission there.

Many years later, after Fray Serra had died, his replacement, Fray Lasuén, suggested building a mission in the area that Fray Crespí had seen. At the time, Mission San Juan Capistrano lay to the north of this valley, and Mission San Diego de Alcalá lay to the south. There were many Native Californian villages in between these two missions. Those wishing to travel between the existing missions felt it was unsafe because it was more than a day's journey, and the Spanish feared that Native people would attack them.

The governor of Alta California, Diego de Borica, agreed with Fray Lasuén that a mission should be founded in the area between the two existing missions to provide Spanish travelers with a safe stopping point. On February 27, 1798, the Spanish government sent soldiers from the San Diego presidio to help build temporary shelters at the site they had chosen for the mission. These dwellings were ready by the time Fray Lasuén dedicated the site on June 13, 1798.

THE FOUNDING OF THE MISSION

The founding ceremony for Mission San Luis Rey de Francia was led by Fray Lasuén, who had made the journey from mission headquarters at San Carlos Borroméo. There to witness the ceremony were Fray Antonio Peyrí, who had come to live at the mission and convert the Native people; Captain Antonio Grajera and his soldiers from the San Diego presidio; Fray Juan Santiago and a few **neophytes**—Native people who had been converted to Christianity—from the nearby Mission San Juan Capistrano; and many

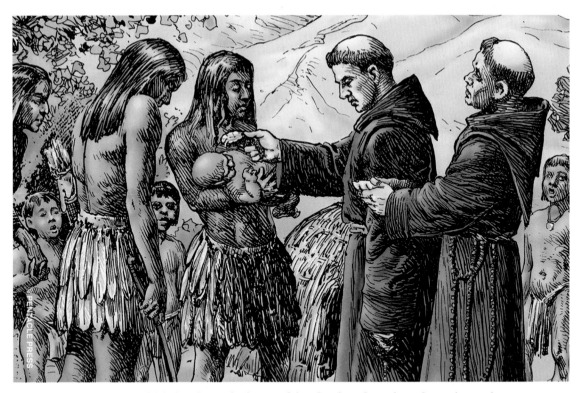

Before a person could join the mission, a friar had to baptize them into the Christian faith.

Luiseño from nearby villages, who were curious to see the event. Some Native people were already aware of the missions in other parts of Alta California, and those who gathered there were about to witness firsthand what a mission in their territory would mean.

Captain Grajera announced to the crowd that he was taking the land "for the crown." This meant that he was taking the land for the king of Spain and that the land would now belong to the Spanish government. Then Fray Lasuén placed a cross in the ground and sprinkled holy water around it, marking it as a sacred spot. Fray Lasuén offered a Mass, or Catholic religious ceremony, and gave a sermon.

After the founding ceremony, Fray Lasuén baptized twenty-nine

Luiseño girls and twenty-five Luiseño boys. **Baptism** is the ceremony that makes someone a Christian. In the Catholic faith, one is usually baptized as a baby or a small child. In addition to the children, nineteen Luiseño adults also asked to be baptized after the founding ceremony, but Fray Lasuén told them that they would have to wait and learn more about the Christian religion first. Since the adults had grown up believing in the Luiseño religion, he felt that they needed to know more about **Catholicism** before they could be baptized. The children were young, so Fray Lasuén baptized them first so that they could grow up as Christians at the mission.

Since Fray Lasuén was in Alta California to convert as many Native people as possible to Christianity, he must have been very pleased with his early success. The missionaries already had many people who wanted to come and live with them at Mission San Luis Rey de Francia, and it was only the first day.

THE FIRST FRIARS

After founding Mission San Luis Rey de Francia, Fray Lasuén remained there for six weeks to help Fray Peyrí, who would be the mission's senior friar once Fray Lasuén left. The two decided on the layout of the mission itself and the surrounding area, including where grain would be planted and where the church and friar's quarters would be built. Shortly after, Fray José Faura arrived at the mission to help Fray Peyrí. Fray Faura taught the Luiseño the Spanish language and the Catholic religion and would oversee the outdoor work.

5
Early Days at the Mission

AN IDEAL LOCATION

The early years at Mission San Luis Rey de Francia were filled with prosperity. This success was largely due to the mission's location, and the tireless efforts of Fray Peyrí.

Like all the mission sites, the site of Mission San Luis Rey de Francia was chosen because it had three important elements: rich soil for growing crops, a convenient water supply, and a large Native Californian population nearby that could be converted to Christianity and made into Spanish citizens.

HUMBLE BEGINNINGS

Fray Peyrí and Fray Faura began their mission with only twelve plowshares, six crowbars, some blankets, pickaxes, and cloth to make clothes for the neophytes, whom they felt needed more appropriate clothing. Food supplies and livestock were sent from nearby missions to help the friars get started. The friars encouraged the Luiseño to work for the mission by giving them food and blankets in return for their labor. Many of these laborers also became neophytes and joined the mission. The friars would teach

Mission San Luis Rey de Francia was the subject of some paintings, like this one drawn by Christian Jörgensen.

the Luiseño people everything they needed to know to become successful builders, farmers, and clothes-makers.

Upon their arrival, the Spanish missionaries and soldiers built temporary huts as quickly as they could. These shelters were constructed mainly from sticks and mud, and were meant to last only until more permanent structures could be built. To make the shelters, branches were placed in the ground to form walls. Then clay was patted into the sticks to make the walls sturdier and to fill in any holes that would have allowed wind or rain to pass through. Roofs were made from sticks, mud, and thatch, a bundle of straw-like reeds and grasses that could be found on the banks of nearby rivers, such as tule. Along with this first group of temporary mission buildings, the missionaries built a chapel from the same basic materials.

STURDY STRUCTURES

Once the temporary shelters were built, the Spanish missionaries could begin to think about all the things they would need in order to create a successful permanent community at the mission.

The permanent buildings that now make up Mission San Luis Rey de Francia took many years to build. Fray Peyrí, also a skilled architect, designed the layout, which was unique to the mission. The mission's walls were made of **adobe** bricks. Masons and artisans came from other missions to teach the Luiseño how to make adobe out of a mixture of mud, straw, and water. This mixture was placed into rectangular wooden molds and left to dry in the sun. Once dry, the bricks could be removed from the molds and stored for later use. By July 1, 1798, less than one month after the mission's founding, 1,000 adobe bricks had been made for the mission's first building, the church, which was completed that same year and served the community until 1802.

A PRODUCTIVE START

Life at Mission San Luis Rey de Francia continued to be busy and productive. On August 29, 1798, Fray Lasuén reported to Governor Borica that 147 Luiseño people had been baptized at Mission San Luis Rey de Francia, and that the friars had married twenty-eight couples in Christian ceremonies. Work was going well, and three rooms of the mission complex were already completed.

Work continued steadily. In 1798, the walls of the friars' quarters and soldiers' **barracks** were finished and had roofs made of thatch and mud. More adobe bricks had been made for the quadrangle—the shape formed when all the main buildings joined together. The walls of the *monjerío*, or living quarters for unmarried women and girls, were finished, but heavy rains prevented the construction of a roof.

In the 1800s, Fray Peyrí allowed smaller sister missions called *asistencias*, as well as villages called *rancherías*, to be built on grassland a few miles away. Built by and for the neophytes, they held livestock, had their own churches, and were operated by other friars. One of San Luis Rey de Francia's asistencias still exists today. It is called the Pala Mission and still serves the local Native community. After converting to Christianity, some Luiseños stayed at the mission, while others returned to their villages. The villages eventually became rancherías full of converted Native people.

By the end of 1798, the mission's first year, 214 neophytes already lived at the mission. The leaders of other missions donated many animals to the mission. The mission's livestock included 162 cows and bulls, 600 sheep, twenty-eight horses, and ten mules. The mission was now prepared to begin farming and ranching. San Luis Rey de Francia was off to a productive start.

Over time, the mission grew to be one of the most successful missions.

6
Daily Life

A TYPICAL DAY

Day to day, Mission San Luis Rey de Francia was full of activity. The community maintained a strict schedule of prayer and work. Bells were rung at sunrise to wake the neophytes, who lived in the monjerío or in adobe dwellings outside the main walls of the mission. Once awake, everyone gathered at the church for morning prayers and to hear Mass. After Mass, the friars taught the neophytes Catholic religious lessons. Everyone then ate breakfast, which was usually a thick corn soup called *atole*.

Following the morning meal, all missionaries, soldiers, and neophytes either went to work or to classes. At noon they all came together again for lunch—usually *pozole*, a vegetable and grain stew served with meat. Following lunch was a *siesta*, or rest period, until 2 p.m. After the siesta, everyone went back to work until sunset, when

This is one of four bells at the mission today.

they gathered again at the church for prayers. After prayers came the evening meal.

It was only after the evening meal that the neophytes were given any free time. During this time, neophytes danced, played instruments and games, and talked together. However, they were forbidden to practice any Native traditions or religious beliefs. Women usually went to bed around 8 p.m., while men went to bed around 9 p.m.

This strict routine ensured that the mission community was very productive. People were always busy doing various jobs: gathering crops, mending walls, making clothes, teaching children, and aiding the sick.

EDUCATION

The education of the neophytes at Mission San Luis Rey de Francia had two goals. One was to teach them a trade or craft that would be useful at the mission, such as leather-making, blacksmithing, weaving, farming, or cooking. These skills were sometimes taught by people from outside the mission, such as tanners and blacksmiths. The other goal was to teach them the Catholic religion and the Spanish language and culture. The friars accomplished this by personally overseeing the neophytes' daily study of the Bible and other Catholic beliefs.

CHORES

Men and women were assigned different tasks. Women usually weaved, washed clothes, cooked, or cleaned. Men tended to crops

While at the mission, everyone had different tasks. Men often learned how to farm, plow, and plant crops.

such as oranges, grapes, wheat, barley, corn, and trees, using wooden plows to till the land and plant their food. In 1830, California's first pepper tree was planted at the mission.

The neophytes also raised cattle for beef and leather, sheep for meat and wool, and hogs for lard, which was used to make soap. Children helped where they could, but spent a lot of time learning from the friars about Christianity and the Spanish language.

LOST FREEDOM

When the Luiseño came to Mission San Luis Rey de Francia, they had to leave behind their own culture and learn an entirely new way of life. Previously accustomed to finding their own food and producing only what the tribe needed, the Luiseño now had to wear new clothes, learn a new language, and live in a new environment. Many did not want to follow the strict schedule at the mission, or produce food and other goods for a much larger community. They were often punished.

Once baptized, the neophytes lost their freedom and had to do what the friars told them to do. Neophytes could not leave the mission grounds (including asistencias) unless they had special permission. If they tried to flee, they were caught and brought back by the soldiers. Runaways were often beaten and punished by the soldiers or friars.

Beginning in 1799, the friars allowed the neophytes to elect *alcaldes*. Alcaldes were neophytes chosen to communicate between the friars and the Native people, and acted as the main authority figures of the neophyte communities. If a person wasn't following the rules, alcaldes had permission to discipline them.

At Mission San Luis Rey de Francia, the neophytes were said to have been treated much better than at any other mission. Fray Peyrí had a kind approach, and many neophytes continued to join the mission. At its peak, in 1825, almost 3,000 people lived on the mission grounds. This was three times the average mission population.

LABOR AT THE MISSION

Although some neophytes disliked taking orders from friars, many stayed and worked at the mission. San Luis Rey de Francia quickly became an economic center. Neophytes built an **irrigation** system to bring water from the springs and river nearby to the mission's *lavandería*, or washing station. Water was used for washing clothes, bathing, and keeping crops healthy.

7
Hardships at the Mission

REVOLUTION AFFECTS THE MISSIONS

Things started to change for the missions of Alta California in 1810, when the Spanish empire went to war with New Spain. Spain had previously sent supplies and money to the friars and soldiers at the missions to sustain them. Now focused on winning the war, the empire could no longer send new supplies or afford to fully pay those Spanish subjects working at the mission. Soldiers were unhappy, and started to take their anger out on the neophytes. This upset the friars, who also complained about being forced to supply food for soldiers at nearby presidios, even though the people at the missions needed it themselves.

During this difficult time, Fray Bartolomé de Carranza, the friar who was now at Mission San Luis Rey de Francia with Fray Peyrí, wrote to Fray Lasuén to ask for permission to return to New Spain. Mission life was difficult, and the friar felt isolated from his home and culture. Fray Lasuén sent a friar named Gerónimo Boscana to replace Fray Carranza. Two more friars, Jayme Escudé and Fray Ramón Oblés, came and went between 1811 and 1823, but Fray Peyrí remained faithful to the mission.

UNREST

1810 sparked more unrest between the friars, the military, and the neophytes. That year, military soldiers insisted on trespassing on mission lands and pasturing horses from the nearby presidio of San Diego at Las Flores, one of Mission San Luis Rey de Francia's asistencias. Fray Peyrí was unhappy, and wrote to the governor, José Arrillaga, to complain.

Meanwhile, the neophytes continued building. In 1811, permission was given for a new church to be constructed. Finished in 1815, it would be the last church built on the mission grounds and was the largest building in Alta California at the time. It was unique because it was one of only two mission churches constructed in the shape of a cross. Famed architect José Antonio Ramirez traveled to the mission to oversee construction and design the new church's roof.

In 1818, problems arose for the missions around the Monterey area. A Frenchman named Hippolyte de Bouchard and a group of pirates threatened to overtake the Santa Barbara presidio. Soldiers and their families living there fled in fear. Many took refuge at Mission San Luis Rey de Francia and its asistencia San Antonio de Pala.

DIVISION OF THE MISSION LANDS

In 1821, fighting between Spain and New Spain ended when New Spain won its independence and became Mexico. The new government brought new changes, especially for the mission system. Mexico at first decided to pass some mission lands back to the newly freed Native people, who would farm the land while Mexican officials and friars ran the missions. However, many officials and settlers were given large pieces of mission land, too, and corrupt ranchers took much of the remaining land from the Natives, leaving some ex-neophytes little choice but to work for them. Outraged, many ex-neophytes left the missions altogether to seek opportunities in the *pueblos* or with Native groups nearby.

The fate of the mission changed after 1821, when Mexico became its own country.

FRAY PEYRÍ LEAVES

This change in control of the mission system also meant Spanish friars who had managed the mission communities for decades were no longer needed. Many were sent back to Spain. In the case of Mission San Luis Rey de Francia, Fray Peyrí stayed for as long as he could, but eventually decided to go back to his native country before the mission was completely destroyed. He did not have the power to stop the

Fray Peyrí blesses the neophytes of Mission San Luis Rey de Francia as they try to swim after his ship.

Mexican government.

In January 1832, after thirty-four years of service, Fray Peyrí left Mission San Luis Rey de Francia under the cover of night. He had tried leaving before, but the neophytes had been so upset they stopped him from leaving. The darkness enabled him to disappear in disguise, and he, along with a few soldiers and two neophytes, traveled to a waiting ship in San Diego's bay.

The following morning, when the neophytes discovered Fray Peyrí was gone, 500 Luiseño mounted their horses and rode to the port of San Diego. They arrived just as Fray Peyrí's ship, the *Pocahontas*, departed.

Fray Peyrí brought two neophytes with him to Spain, Pablo Tac and Agapito Amamix. While both went on to Rome to become friars, they unfortunately fell ill and died before they could complete their training. However, Pablo Tac, a promising young priest, wrote a detailed account of his life at Mission San Luis Rey de Francia and documented more than 1,200 words from the Luiseño language before his death in 1841.

8
Secularization

SECULARIZATION OF THE MISSION

The process of handing control of the missions from the Catholic friars to the Mexican government was known as **secularization**. In 1826, the governor, José María de Echeandía, began secularization by freeing the neophytes from the friars' control. However, the indigenous people still had to obey Mexican government officials.

On January 6, 1831, Governor Echeandía appointed a military officer named Captain Pablo de la Portilla to divide up the lands surrounding Mission San Luis Rey de Francia. He was told to give 33 acres (13.4 hectares) to each adult male over twenty years of age. The Mexican government had made it legal to force the California Natives to work in the fields, and Captain Portilla tried to enforce this at Mission San Luis Rey de Francia. However, after a month at the mission he reported that the ex-neophytes were not listening to him. Many left to find opportunities elsewhere.

In 1833, the government passed laws that called for immediate secularization of all missions, which turned them into towns, called pueblos. Mission San Luis Rey de Francia was officially secularized and handed over to administrators in 1834. These administrators divided the land among themselves, leaving almost nothing to the Luiseño people.

DISORDER AT THE MISSION

Secularization caused many problems at Mission San Luis Rey de Francia. Two friars, Fray Antonio Ánzar and Fray Vicente Pasqual Oliva, had been sent to take Fray Peyrí's place as leaders of the mission. They quickly discovered that most of the neophytes had left, and those remaining refused to do the work the friars felt was necessary to save the mission. Fray Oliva became depressed and almost crazed—there was no order at the mission, and things were going very badly.

LIFE AFTER SECULARIZATION

In 1846, Mission San Luis Rey de Francia was sold by a new Mexican governor named Pio Pico to members of his family. It

was stripped of all its valuable goods, which were used to build settlers' houses. It was occupied during the Mexican–American War in the 1840s and 1850s, when U.S. troops, including the Mormon Battalion, lived there. They used the church as a stable for horses and other animals.

The mission finally became part of the United States in 1850 when California became a state. The United States had won the Mexican–American War, and claimed this territory as part of its victory. In the 1860s, the missions were given back to the Catholic Church to manage. Mission San Luis Rey de Francia would face neglect until 1892, when a Franciscan priest named Joseph Jeremiah O'Keefe began restoring it for use as a Franciscan missionary college.

The neophytes living at the mission refused to work for government officials and friars who took over from Fray Peyrí.

Today the mission has been restored and is a **National Historic Landmark** attracting many visitors each year.

9
The Mission Today

RESTORING THE MISSION

Fray O'Keefe and his order of Mexican missionaries, the Zacatecas, found a new home at Mission San Luis Rey de Francia. On May 12, 1893, Bishop Mora rededicated the mission. For the next nineteen years, Fray O'Keefe oversaw the mission's **restoration**. Even after his death in 1915, reconstruction continued.

THE LANDMARK MISSION

By the 1920s and 1930s, the Franciscans had restored the mission enough to allow movies to be filmed there. Films and TV shows such as *The Pride of Palomar* (1922) and *Zorro* (1957) were shot at Mission San Luis Rey de Francia, and it quickly became a tourist attraction. By 1931, the church again closely resembled its original design. Restoration of the soldiers' barracks and the lavandería took place in the 1950s and 1960s. In 1970, the United States Department of the Interior made the mission a National Historic Landmark. Today, there are ongoing efforts to restore many paintings and other artifacts that are part the mission's rich past.

PRESERVING THE PAST

Mission San Luis Rey de Francia continues today as a working mission. The land around it has changed a lot over the years. A far cry from its original size of over 950,000 acres (384,451 ha), the property today sits on fifty-six acres (22 ha) and serves the local community as a tourist attraction, a church, and a retreat center. Masses are held every weekend in the mission church, where the copper baptismal font made by the neophytes is still displayed.

On what once was the friars' living quarters now stands a museum dedicated to the mission's history. Items there include Luiseño baskets, **vestments** worn by the eighteenth- and nineteenth-century friars, works of art, and a display of the mission kitchen. It contains artifacts from all periods of the mission's life, beginning with the Luiseño people before the Spanish arrived.

THE CEMETERY

Mission San Luis Rey de Francia has its own cemetery that dates back to 1798. It is the oldest burial ground still used in North San Diego County. A memorial built in 1830 is in memory of the Luiseño people who built the mission and for the many who died there.

MISSION SAN LUIS REY DE FRANCIA'S LEGACY

The mission is a lasting reminder of one of the most transformative eras of California's history. It was part of a system that brought settlers to California and made it what it is today. However, this same system also changed the lives of thousands of Native Californians. It is a fascinating place to visit and to explore.

10
Make Your Own Mission Model

To make your own model of the San Luis Rey de Francia mission, you will need:

- Corrugated cardboard
- scissors
- Foam Core board
- Scotch® tape
- ruler
- glue
- light brown paint

- reddish brown paint
- green and white paint
- paint brushes
- miniature pots
- greenery
- wire
- miniature bell

DIRECTIONS

Adult supervision is suggested.

Step 1: Use a large piece of the corrugated cardboard for your base.

Step 2: Cut out two pieces of Foam Core that are 8"× 3" (20.3 cm × 7.6 cm) and two pieces that are 6"× 3" (15.2 cm × 7.6 cm).

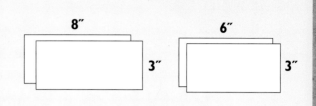

Step 3: Carefully cut arches in one of the 8"× 3" (20.3 cm × 7.6 cm) pieces of Foam Core to make the front of your mission.

Step 4: Arrange the remaining Foam Core pieces around the base so they form a box shape. Tape them together. Attach to the mission base.

Step 5: Cut out twelve pieces of Foam Core that are 3"× 2" (7.6 cm × 5.1 cm) and six pieces that are 3"× 1.5" (7.6 cm × 3.8 cm).

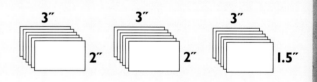

Step 6: Tape two pieces of the Foam Core that are 3"× 2" (7.6 cm × 5.1 cm) and one piece that is 3"× 1.5" (7.6 cm × 3.8 cm) into three sides of a box. Repeat with all pieces to form six three-sided boxes.

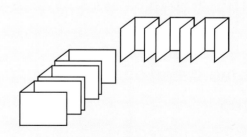

Step 7: Tape three of these box shapes to the right side of the building and three along the back, as shown.

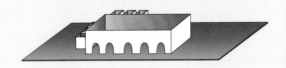

Step 8: To make the church buildings and steeple, cut out four Foam Core board pieces that are 3"× 3" (7.6 cm × 7.6 cm) and eight that are 1.5"× 3" (3.8 cm × 7.6 cm).

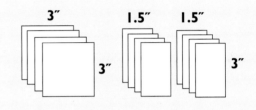

Step 9: Tape together two Foam Core board pieces that are 3"× 3" (7.6 cm × 7.6 cm) and one piece that is 1.5"× 3" (3.8 cm × 7.6 cm) to form three sides of a box. Attach to the left side of the mission.

Step 10: Tape together two pieces of 3" × 3" (7.6 cm × 7.6 cm) Foam Core board and three pieces that are 1.5"× 3" (3.8 cm × 7.6 cm) to form an "L" shape. Attach the "L" shape to the right side of the church.

Step 11: To make the church steeple, use the remaining four pieces that are 1.5"× 3" (3.8 cm × 7.6 cm). Tape together in a square and place on top of the first box.

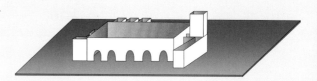

Step 12: Cut out two pieces of Foam Core board that are 3"× 3" (7.6 cm × 7.6 cm) and one piece that is 2"× 3" (5.1 cm × 7.6 cm). Tape these into three sides of a box and attach to front, right side of the main building.

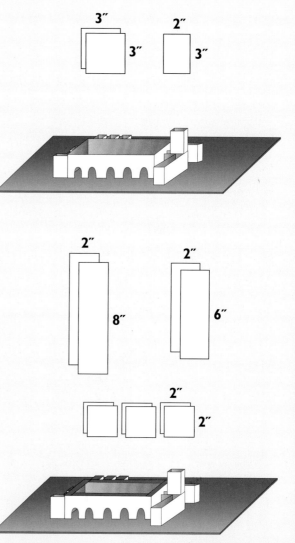

Step 13: To make the roofs, cut out two pieces of corrugated cardboard that are 2"× 8" (5.1 cm × 20.3 cm) and two pieces that are 2"× 6" (5.1 cm × 15.2 cm) for the main building. For the small buildings, cut out corrugated cardboard roofs that are 2"× 2" (5.1 cm × 5.1 cm).

Step 14: For the church, cut out two corrugated cardboard roofs that are 1.5" × 1.5" (3.8 cm × 3.8 cm). For the church steeple, cut a piece that is 2" × 4" (5.1 cm × 10.2 cm) and fold in half. Attach all pieces and glue in place. Let the model dry completely.

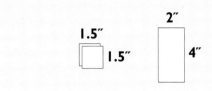

Step 15: Attach a bell to the steeple. Add miniature pots and fill with greenery. Paint your mission as you wish.

The model of Mission San Luis Rey de Francia when it is completed.

Key Dates in Mission History

1492   Christopher Columbus reaches the West Indies

1542   Cabrillo's expedition to California

1602   Sebastián Vizcaíno sails to California

1713   Fray Junípero Serra is born

1769   Founding of San Diego de Alcalá

1770   Founding of San Carlos Borroméo del Río Carmelo

1771   Founding of San Antonio de Padua and
San Gabriel Arcángel

1772   Founding of San Luis Obispo de Tolosa

1775–76   Founding of San Juan Capistrano

1776   Founding of San Francisco de Asís

1776   Declaration of Independence is signed

1777	Founding of Santa Clara de Asís
1782	Founding of San Buenaventura
1784	Fray Serra dies
1786	Founding of Santa Bárbara
1787	Founding of La Purísima Concepción
1791	Founding of Santa Cruz and Nuestra Señora de la Soledad
1797	Founding of San José, San Juan Bautista, San Miguel Arcángel, and San Fernando Rey de España
1798	Founding of San Luis Rey de Francia
1804	Founding of Santa Inés
1817	Founding of San Rafael Arcángel
1823	Founding of San Francisco Solano
1833	Mexico passes Secularization Act
1848	Gold found in northern California
1850	California becomes the thirty-first state

Glossary

adobe (uh-DOH-bee)
Sun-dried bricks made of straw, mud, and sometimes manure.

baptism (BAP-tih-zum)
A ceremony performed when someone is accepted into, or accepts, the Christian faith.

barracks (BAYR-iks)
A building or set of buildings that are used to house soldiers.

Catholicism (kuh-THAH-lih-sih-zum) The faith or practice of Catholic Christianity, which includes following the spiritual leadership of priests headed by the pope.

Christianity (kris-chee-AH-nih-tee) A religion based on the teachings of Jesus Christ and the Bible, practiced by Eastern, Roman Catholic, and Protestant groups.

convert (kun-VIRT)
To change from belief in one religion to belief in another religion.

Franciscan (fran-SIS-kin)
A communal Roman Catholic order of friars, or "brothers," who follow the teachings and example of Saint Francis of Assisi, who did much work as a missionary.

friar (FRY-ur)
A brother in a communal religious order. Friars can also be priests.

indigenous people (in-DIJ-en-us PEA-pel)
People native born to a particular region or environment.

irrigation (eer-ih-GAY-shun)
A system devised to supply an area with water.

neophyte (NEE-oh-fyt)
The name for an indigenous
person baptized into the
Christian faith.

restoration (reh-stuh-RAY-
shun) Working to return
something, such as a building,
to its original state.

secularization (seh-kyoo-
luh-rih-ZAY-shun) When the
operation of the mission lands
was turned over to the Mexican
government.

vestments (VEST-mints)
Robes that are worn for special
ceremonies.

viceroy (VYS-roy) A governor
who rules and acts as the repre-
sentative of the king.

Pronunciation Guide

alcaldes (ahl-KAHL-des)

fray (FRAY)

lavandería (lah-ban-deh-REE-ah)

monjerío (mohn-hay-REE-oh)

pauhits (POW-eetz)

pueblos (PWAY-blohz)

ranchería (rahn-cheh-REE-ah)

siesta (see-EHS-tah)

wamkish (WAHM-kish)

Find Out More

To learn more about the California missions, check out these books and websites:

BOOKS

Gendell, Megan. *The Spanish Missions of California*. New York, NY: True Books, 2010.

Lemke, Nancy. *Southern Coast Missions of California*. Minneapolis, MN: Lerner Publishing, 2008.

Levick, Melba, Stanley Young, and Sally B. Woodridge. *The Missions of California*. San Francisco, CA: Chronicle Books, 2004.

Padelsky, Londie. *California Missions*. Ketchum, ID: Stoecklein Publishing, 2006.

WEBSITES

California Missions Foundation

www.californiamissionsfoundation.org

This website provides a timeline, historical information, as well as current news on ongoing mission renovation projects.

California Missions Resource Center

www.missionscalifornia.com

This website gives essential facts about each mission. It also provides a timeline and a photo gallery.

Official Website of Mission San Luis Rey de Francia

www.sanluisrey.org

This website contains historical information and an updated listing of Mission San Luis Rey de Francia's workshops, retreats, museum hours, and more.

Index